KAKEIBO

THE JAPANESE
OF ART
SAVING MONEY

Monthly Income

Source	Data	Amount

Total T1

Fixed Monthly Expenses

Mortgage		Bills(Electric,Gas,Water)		
Insurance		Phone		
Credits		Internet		

Total T2

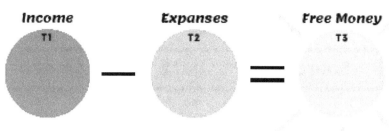

Week 1	General (transport, food, medicine, etc)	Rest (entertaiment, restaurant, club, etc)	Culture (books, education, exhibition, etc)	Unexpected (gifts, repairs, etc)
Monday				
Tuesday				
Wednesday				
Thursday				
Friday				
Saturday				
Sanday				
Total				

Week 2	General (transport, food, medicine, etc)	Rest (entertaiment, restaurant, club, etc)	Culture (books, education, exhibition, etc)	Unexpected (gifts, repairs, etc)
Monday				
Tuesday				
Wednesday				
Thursday				
Friday				
Saturday				
Sanday				
Total				

Week 3	General (transport, food, medicine, etc)	Rest (entertaiment, restaurant, club, etc)	Culture (books, education, exhibition, etc)	Unexpected (gifts, repairs, etc)
Monday				
Tuesday				
Wednesday				
Thursday				
Friday				
Saturday				
Sanday				
Total				

Week 4	General (transport, food, medicine, etc)	Rest (entertaiment, restaurant, club, etc)	Culture (books, education, exhibition, etc)	Unexpected (gifts, repairs, etc)
Monday				
Tuesday				
Wednesday				
Thursday				
Friday				
Saturday				
Sanday				
Total				

Week 5	General (transport, food, medicine, etc)	Rest (entertaiment, restaurant, club, etc)	Culture (books, education, exhibition, etc)	Unexpected (gifts, repairs, etc)
Monday				
Tuesday				
Wednesday				
Thursday				
Friday				
Saturday				
Sanday				
Total				

Week 6	General (transport, food, medicine, etc)	Rest (entertaiment, restaurant, club, etc)	Culture (books, education, exhibition, etc)	Unexpected (gifts, repairs, etc)
Monday				
Tuesday				
Total				

	General	Rest	Culture	Unexpected
Week 1				
Week 2				
Week 3				
Week 4				
Week 5				
Week 6				
Total				

Month total $_{T7}$

Free Money $_{T3}$ — Month total $_{T7}$ = Save Money

Monthly Income

Source	Data	Amount

Total $_{T1}$

Fixed Monthly Expenses

Category	Amount	Category	Amount
Mortgage		Bills (Electric, Gas, Water)	
Insurance		Phone	
Credits		Internet	

Total $_{T2}$

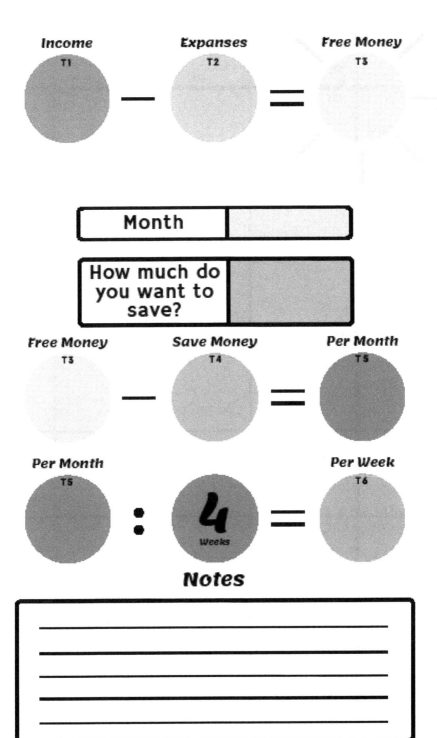

Week 1	General (transport, food, medicine, etc)	Rest (entertaiment, restaurant, club, etc)	Culture (books, education, exhibition, etc)	Unexpected (gifts, repairs, etc)
Monday				
Tuesday				
Wednesday				
Thursday				
Friday				
Saturday				
Sanday				
Total				

Week 2	General (transport, food, medicine, etc)	Rest (entertaiment, restaurant, club, etc)	Culture (books, education, exhibition, etc)	Unexpected (gifts, repairs, etc)
Monday				
Tuesday				
Wednesday				
Thursday				
Friday				
Saturday				
Sanday				
Total				

Week 3	General (transport, food, medicine, etc)	Rest (entertaiment, restaurant, club, etc)	Culture (books, education, exhibition, etc)	Unexpected (gifts, repairs, etc)
Monday				
Tuesday				
Wednesday				
Thursday				
Friday				
Saturday				
Sanday				
Total				

Week 4	General (transport, food, medicine, etc)	Rest (entertaiment, restaurant, club, etc)	Culture (books, education, exhibition, etc)	Unexpected (gifts, repairs, etc)
Monday				
Tuesday				
Wednesday				
Thursday				
Friday				
Saturday				
Sanday				
Total				

Week 5	General (transport, food, medicine, etc)	Rest (entertaiment, restaurant, club, etc)	Culture (books, education, exhibition, etc)	Unexpected (gifts, repairs, etc)
Monday				
Tuesday				
Wednesday				
Thursday				
Friday				
Saturday				
Sanday				
Total				

Week 6	General (transport, food, medicine, etc)	Rest (entertaiment, restaurant, club, etc)	Culture (books, education, exhibition, etc)	Unexpected (gifts, repairs, etc)
Monday				
Tuesday				
Total				

	General	Rest	Culture	Unexpected
Week 1				
Week 2				
Week 3				
Week 4				
Week 5				
Week 6				
Total				

Month total $_{T7}$

Free Money $_{T3}$ — Month total $_{T7}$ = Save Money

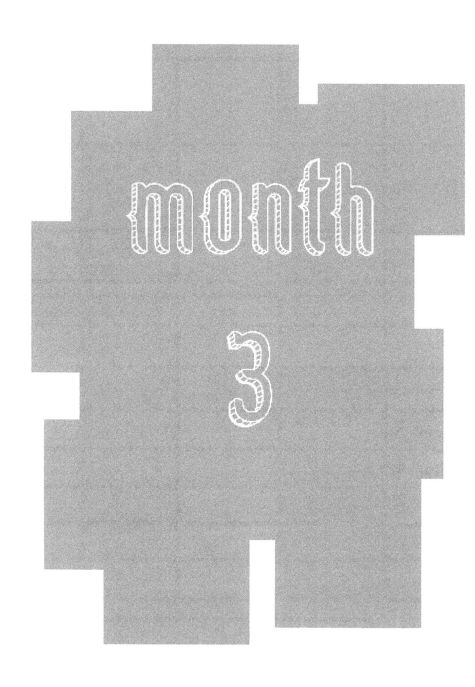

Monthly Income

Source	Data	Amount

Total $_{T1}$

Fixed Monthly Expenses

Mortgage		Bills(Electric,Gas,Water)	
Insurance		Phone	
Credits		Internet	

Total $_{T2}$

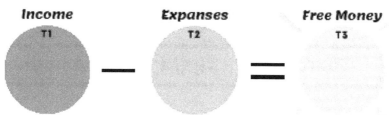

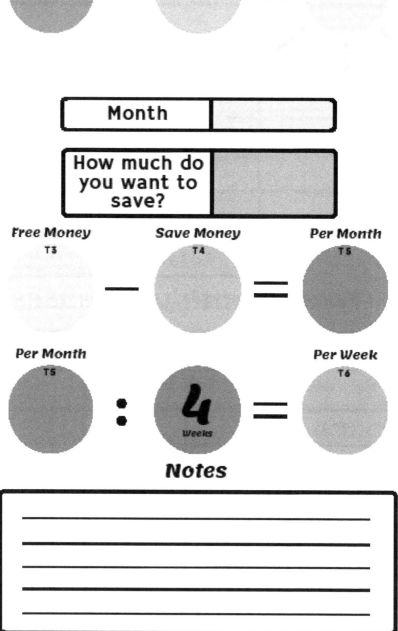

Notes

Week 1	General (transport, food, medicine, etc)	Rest (entertaiment, restaurant, club, etc)	Culture (books, education, exhibition, etc)	Unexpected (gifts, repairs, etc)
Monday				
Tuesday				
Wednesday				
Thursday				
Friday				
Saturday				
Sanday				
Total				

Week 2	General (transport, food, medicine, etc)	Rest (entertaiment, restaurant, club, etc)	Culture (books, education, exhibition, etc)	Unexpected (gifts, repairs, etc)
Monday				
Tuesday				
Wednesday				
Thursday				
Friday				
Saturday				
Sanday				
Total				

Week 3	General (transport, food, medicine, etc)	Rest (entertaiment, restaurant, club, etc)	Culture (books, education, exhibition, etc)	Unexpected (gifts, repairs, etc)
Monday				
Tuesday				
Wednesday				
Thursday				
Friday				
Saturday				
Sanday				
Total				

Week 4	General (transport, food, medicine, etc)	Rest (entertaiment, restaurant, club, etc)	Culture (books, education, exhibition, etc)	Unexpected (gifts, repairs, etc)
Monday				
Tuesday				
Wednesday				
Thursday				
Friday				
Saturday				
Sanday				
Total				

Week 5	General (transport, food, medicine, etc)	Rest (entertaiment, restaurant, club, etc)	Culture (books, education, exhibition, etc)	Unexpected (gifts, repairs, etc)
Monday				
Tuesday				
Wednesday				
Thursday				
Friday				
Saturday				
Sanday				
Total				

Week 6	General (transport, food, medicine, etc)	Rest (entertaiment, restaurant, club, etc)	Culture (books, education, exhibition, etc)	Unexpected (gifts, repairs, etc)
Monday				
Tuesday				
Total				

	General	Rest	Culture	Unexpected
Week 1				
Week 2				
Week 3				
Week 4				
Week 5				
Week 6				
Total				

Month total $_{T7}$

Free Money $_{T3}$ — Month total $_{T7}$ = Save Money

Monthly Income

Source	Data	Amount

Total T1

Fixed Monthly Expenses

Mortgage		Bills(Electric,Gas,Water)	
Insurance		Phone	
Credits		Internet	

Total T2

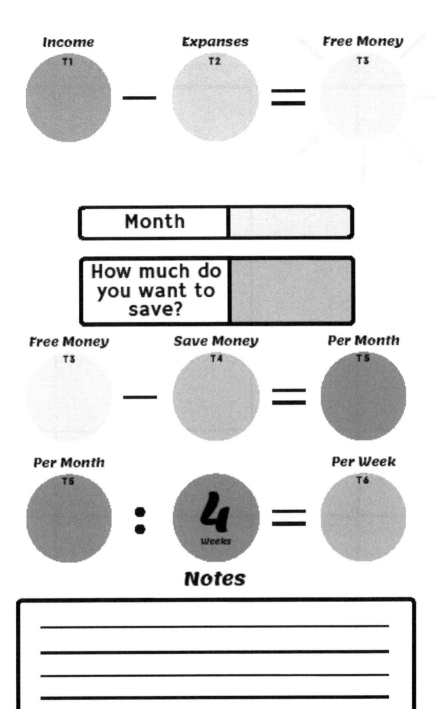

Week 1	General (transport, food, medicine, etc)	Rest (entertaiment, restaurant, club, etc)	Culture (books, education, exhibition, etc)	Unexpected (gifts, repairs, etc)
Monday				
Tuesday				
Wednesday				
Thursday				
Friday				
Saturday				
Sanday				
Total				

Week 2	General (transport, food, medicine, etc)	Rest (entertaiment, restaurant, club, etc)	Culture (books, education, exhibition, etc)	Unexpected (gifts, repairs, etc)
Monday				
Tuesday				
Wednesday				
Thursday				
Friday				
Saturday				
Sanday				
Total				

Week 3	General (transport, food, medicine, etc)	Rest (entertaiment, restaurant, club, etc)	Culture (books, education, exhibition, etc)	Unexpected (gifts, repairs, etc)
Monday				
Tuesday				
Wednesday				
Thursday				
Friday				
Saturday				
Sanday				
Total				

Week 4	General (transport, food, medicine, etc)	Rest (entertaiment, restaurant, club, etc)	Culture (books, education, exhibition, etc)	Unexpected (gifts, repairs, etc)
Monday				
Tuesday				
Wednesday				
Thursday				
Friday				
Saturday				
Sanday				
Total				

Week 5	General (transport, food, medicine, etc)	Rest (entertaiment, restaurant, club, etc)	Culture (books, education, exhibition, etc)	Unexpected (gifts, repairs, etc)
Monday				
Tuesday				
Wednesday				
Thursday				
Friday				
Saturday				
Sanday				
Total				

Week 6	General (transport, food, medicine, etc)	Rest (entertaiment, restaurant, club, etc)	Culture (books, education, exhibition, etc)	Unexpected (gifts, repairs, etc)
Monday				
Tuesday				
Total				

	General	Rest	Culture	Unexpected
Week 1				
Week 2				
Week 3				
Week 4				
Week 5				
Week 6				
Total				

Month total $_{T7}$

Free Money $_{T3}$ — Month total $_{T7}$ = Save Money

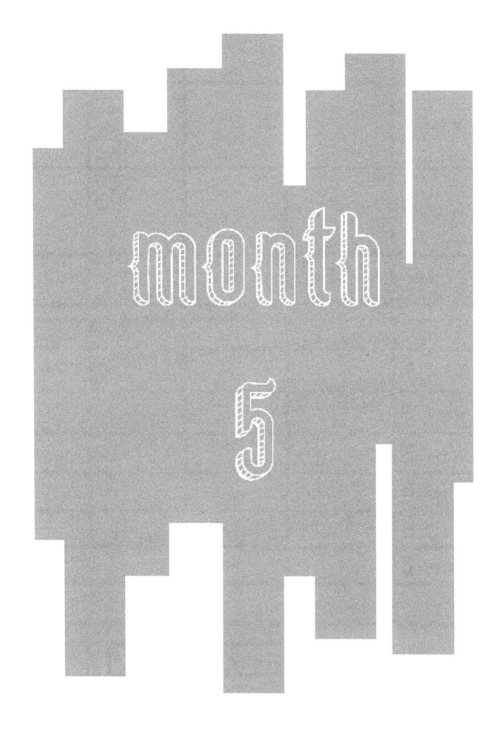

Monthly Income

Source	Data	Amount

Total $_{T1}$

Fixed Monthly Expenses

Mortgage		Bills(Electric,Gas,Water)	
Insurance		Phone	
Credits		Internet	

Total $_{T2}$

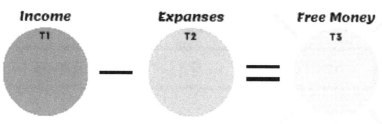
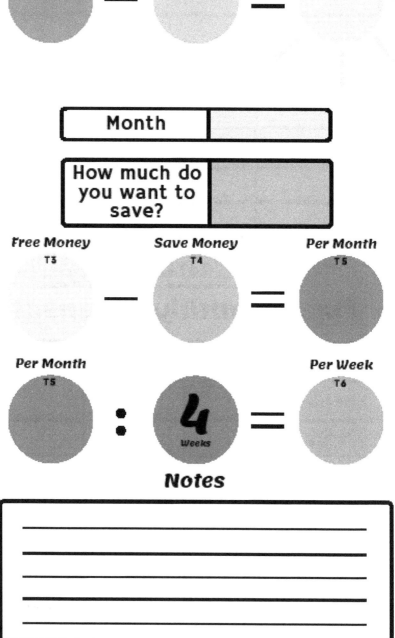

Week 1	General (transport, food, medicine, etc)	Rest (entertaiment, restaurant, club, etc)	Culture (books, education, exhibition, etc)	Unexpected (gifts, repairs, etc)
Monday				
Tuesday				
Wednesday				
Thursday				
Friday				
Saturday				
Sanday				
Total				

Week 2	General (transport, food, medicine, etc)	Rest (entertaiment, restaurant, club, etc)	Culture (books, education, exhibition, etc)	Unexpected (gifts, repairs, etc)
Monday				
Tuesday				
Wednesday				
Thursday				
Friday				
Saturday				
Sanday				
Total				

Week 3	General (transport, food, medicine, etc)	Rest (entertaiment, restaurant, club, etc)	Culture (books, education, exhibition, etc)	Unexpected (gifts, repairs, etc)
Monday				
Tuesday				
Wednesday				
Thursday				
Friday				
Saturday				
Sanday				
Total				

Week 4	General (transport, food, medicine, etc)	Rest (entertaiment, restaurant, club, etc)	Culture (books, education, exhibition, etc)	Unexpected (gifts, repairs, etc)
Monday				
Tuesday				
Wednesday				
Thursday				
Friday				
Saturday				
Sanday				
Total				

Week 5	General (transport, food, medicine, etc)	Rest (entertaiment, restaurant, club, etc)	Culture (books, education, exhibition, etc)	Unexpected (gifts, repairs, etc)
Monday				
Tuesday				
Wednesday				
Thursday				
Friday				
Saturday				
Sanday				
Total				

Week 6	General (transport, food, medicine, etc)	Rest (entertaiment, restaurant, club, etc)	Culture (books, education, exhibition, etc)	Unexpected (gifts, repairs, etc)
Monday				
Tuesday				
Total				

	General	Rest	Culture	Unexpected
Week 1				
Week 2				
Week 3				
Week 4				
Week 5				
Week 6				
Total				

Month total $_{T7}$

Free Money $_{T3}$ — Month total $_{T7}$ = Save Money

Monthly Income

Source	Data	Amount

Total T1

Fixed Monthly Expenses

Mortgage		Bills(Electric,Gas,Water)	
Insurance		Phone	
Credits		Internet	

Total T2

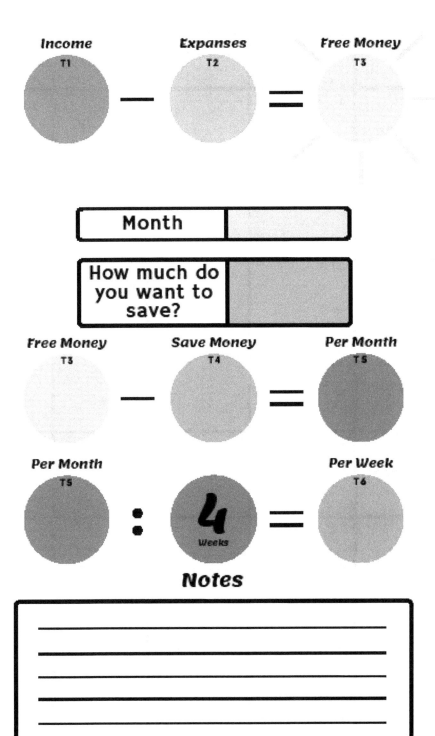

Week 1	General (transport, food, medicine, etc)	Rest (entertaiment, restaurant, club, etc)	Culture (books, education, exhibition, etc)	Unexpected (gifts, repairs, etc)
Monday				
Tuesday				
Wednesday				
Thursday				
Friday				
Saturday				
Sanday				
Total				

Week 2	General (transport, food, medicine, etc)	Rest (entertaiment, restaurant, club, etc)	Culture (books, education, exhibition, etc)	Unexpected (gifts, repairs, etc)
Monday				
Tuesday				
Wednesday				
Thursday				
Friday				
Saturday				
Sanday				
Total				

Week 3	General (transport, food, medicine, etc)	Rest (entertaiment, restaurant, club, etc)	Culture (books, education, exhibition, etc)	Unexpected (gifts, repairs, etc)
Monday				
Tuesday				
Wednesday				
Thursday				
Friday				
Saturday				
Sanday				
Total				

Week 4	General (transport, food, medicine, etc)	Rest (entertaiment, restaurant, club, etc)	Culture (books, education, exhibition, etc)	Unexpected (gifts, repairs, etc)
Monday				
Tuesday				
Wednesday				
Thursday				
Friday				
Saturday				
Sanday				
Total				

Week 5	General (transport, food, medicine, etc)	Rest (entertaiment, restaurant, club, etc)	Culture (books, education, exhibition, etc)	Unexpected (gifts, repairs, etc)
Monday				
Tuesday				
Wednesday				
Thursday				
Friday				
Saturday				
Sanday				
Total				

Week 6	General (transport, food, medicine, etc)	Rest (entertaiment, restaurant, club, etc)	Culture (books, education, exhibition, etc)	Unexpected (gifts, repairs, etc)
Monday				
Tuesday				
Total				

	General	Rest	Culture	Unexpected
Week 1				
Week 2				
Week 3				
Week 4				
Week 5				
Week 6				
Total				

Month total $_{T7}$

Free Money $_{T3}$ — Month total $_{T7}$ = Save Money

Monthly Income

Source	Data	Amount

Total T1

Fixed Monthly Expenses

Mortgage		Bills(Electric,Gas,Water)	
Insurance		Phone	
Credits		Internet	

Total T2

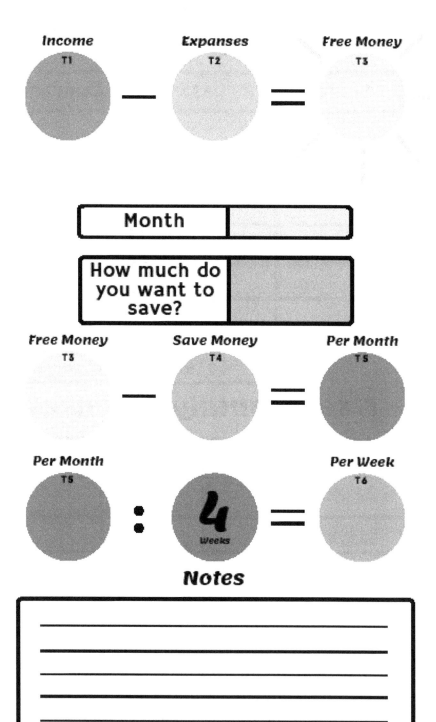

Week 1	General (transport, food, medicine, etc)	Rest (entertaiment, restaurant, club, etc)	Culture (books, education, exhibition, etc)	Unexpected (gifts, repairs, etc)
Monday				
Tuesday				
Wednesday				
Thursday				
Friday				
Saturday				
Sanday				
Total				

Week 2	General (transport, food, medicine, etc)	Rest (entertaiment, restaurant, club, etc)	Culture (books, education, exhibition, etc)	Unexpected (gifts, repairs, etc)
Monday				
Tuesday				
Wednesday				
Thursday				
Friday				
Saturday				
Sanday				
Total				

Week 3	General (transport, food, medicine, etc)	Rest (entertaiment, restaurant, club, etc)	Culture (books, education, exhibition, etc)	Unexpected (gifts, repairs, etc)
Monday				
Tuesday				
Wednesday				
Thursday				
Friday				
Saturday				
Sanday				
Total				

Week 4	General (transport, food, medicine, etc)	Rest (entertaiment, restaurant, club, etc)	Culture (books, education, exhibition, etc)	Unexpected (gifts, repairs, etc)
Monday				
Tuesday				
Wednesday				
Thursday				
Friday				
Saturday				
Sanday				
Total				

Week 5	General (transport, food, medicine, etc)	Rest (entertaiment, restaurant, club, etc)	Culture (books, education, exhibition, etc)	Unexpected (gifts, repairs, etc)
Monday				
Tuesday				
Wednesday				
Thursday				
Friday				
Saturday				
Sanday				
Total				

Week 6	General (transport, food, medicine, etc)	Rest (entertaiment, restaurant, club, etc)	Culture (books, education, exhibition, etc)	Unexpected (gifts, repairs, etc)
Monday				
Tuesday				
Total				

	General	Rest	Culture	Unexpected
Week 1				
Week 2				
Week 3				
Week 4				
Week 5				
Week 6				
Total				

Month total $_{T7}$

Free Money $_{T3}$ — Month total $_{T7}$ = Save Money

Monthly Income

Source	Data	Amount

Total T1

Fixed Monthly Expenses

Mortgage		Bills(Electric,Gas, Water)	
Insurance		Phone	
Credits		Internet	

Total T2

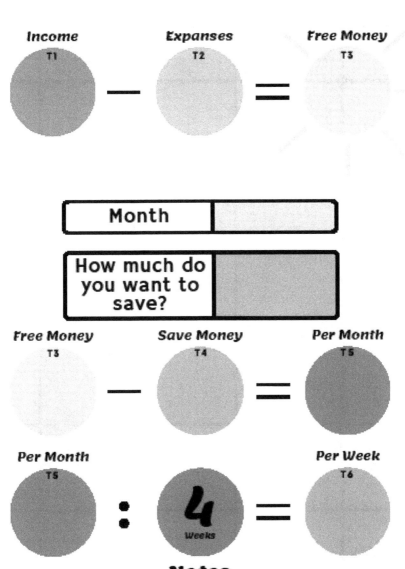

Week 1	General (transport, food, medicine, etc)	Rest (entertaiment, restaurant, club, etc)	Culture (books, education, exhibition, etc)	Unexpected (gifts, repairs, etc)
Monday				
Tuesday				
Wednesday				
Thursday				
Friday				
Saturday				
Sanday				
Total				

Week 2	General (transport, food, medicine, etc)	Rest (entertaiment, restaurant, club, etc)	Culture (books, education, exhibition, etc)	Unexpected (gifts, repairs, etc)
Monday				
Tuesday				
Wednesday				
Thursday				
Friday				
Saturday				
Sanday				
Total				

Week 3	General (transport, food, medicine, etc)	Rest (entertaiment, restaurant, club, etc)	Culture (books, education, exhibition, etc)	Unexpected (gifts, repairs, etc)
Monday				
Tuesday				
Wednesday				
Thursday				
Friday				
Saturday				
Sanday				
Total				

Week 4	General (transport, food, medicine, etc)	Rest (entertaiment, restaurant, club, etc)	Culture (books, education, exhibition, etc)	Unexpected (gifts, repairs, etc)
Monday				
Tuesday				
Wednesday				
Thursday				
Friday				
Saturday				
Sanday				
Total				

Week 5	General (transport, food, medicine, etc)	Rest (entertaiment, restaurant, club, etc)	Culture (books, education, exhibition, etc)	Unexpected (gifts, repairs, etc)
Monday				
Tuesday				
Wednesday				
Thursday				
Friday				
Saturday				
Sanday				
Total				

Week 6	General (transport, food, medicine, etc)	Rest (entertaiment, restaurant, club, etc)	Culture (books, education, exhibition, etc)	Unexpected (gifts, repairs, etc)
Monday				
Tuesday				
Total				

	General	Rest	Culture	Unexpected
Week 1				
Week 2				
Week 3				
Week 4				
Week 5				
Week 6				
Total				

Month total $_{T7}$

Free Money $_{T3}$ — Month total $_{T7}$ = Save Money

Monthly Income

Source	Data	Amount

Total $_{T1}$

Fixed Monthly Expenses

Mortgage		Bills(Electric,Gas,Water)	
Insurance		Phone	
Credits		Internet	

Total $_{T2}$

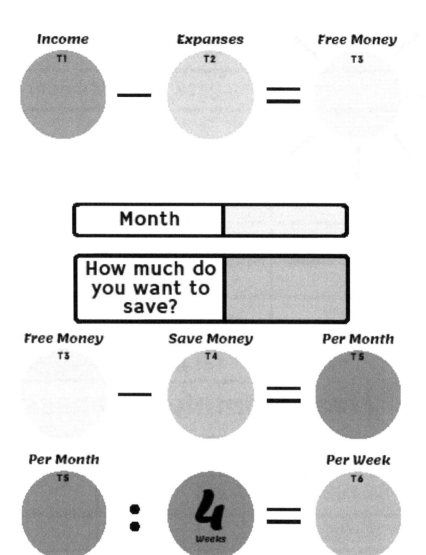

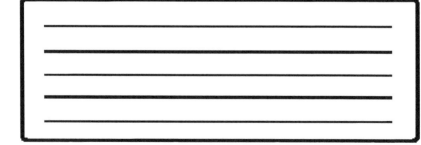

Week 1	General (transport, food, medicine, etc)	Rest (entertaiment, restaurant, club, etc)	Culture (books, education, exhibition, etc)	Unexpected (gifts, repairs, etc)
Monday				
Tuesday				
Wednesday				
Thursday				
Friday				
Saturday				
Sanday				
Total				

Week 2	General (transport, food, medicine, etc)	Rest (entertaiment, restaurant, club, etc)	Culture (books, education, exhibition, etc)	Unexpected (gifts, repairs, etc)
Monday				
Tuesday				
Wednesday				
Thursday				
Friday				
Saturday				
Sanday				
Total				

Week 3	General (transport, food, medicine, etc)	Rest (entertaiment, restaurant, club, etc)	Culture (books, education, exhibition, etc)	Unexpected (gifts, repairs, etc)
Monday				
Tuesday				
Wednesday				
Thursday				
Friday				
Saturday				
Sanday				
Total				

Week 4	General (transport, food, medicine, etc)	Rest (entertaiment, restaurant, club, etc)	Culture (books, education, exhibition, etc)	Unexpected (gifts, repairs, etc)
Monday				
Tuesday				
Wednesday				
Thursday				
Friday				
Saturday				
Sanday				
Total				

Week 5	General (transport, food, medicine, etc)	Rest (entertaiment, restaurant, club, etc)	Culture (books, education, exhibition, etc)	Unexpected (gifts, repairs, etc)
Monday				
Tuesday				
Wednesday				
Thursday				
Friday				
Saturday				
Sanday				
Total				

Week 6	General (transport, food, medicine, etc)	Rest (entertaiment, restaurant, club, etc)	Culture (books, education, exhibition, etc)	Unexpected (gifts, repairs, etc)
Monday				
Tuesday				
Total				

	General	Rest	Culture	Unexpected
Week 1				
Week 2				
Week 3				
Week 4				
Week 5				
Week 6				
Total				

Month total $_{T7}$

Free Money $_{T3}$ — Month total $_{T7}$ = Save Money

Monthly Income

Source	Data	Amount

Total $_{T1}$

Fixed Monthly Expenses

Mortgage		Bills(Electric, Gas, Water)	
Insurance		Phone	
Credits		Internet	

Total $_{T2}$

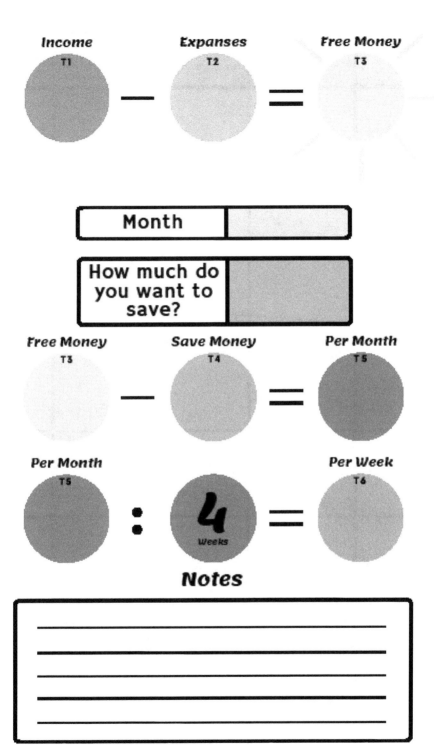

Week 1	General (transport, food, medicine, etc)	Rest (entertaiment, restaurant, club, etc)	Culture (books, education, exhibition, etc)	Unexpected (gifts, repairs, etc)
Monday				
Tuesday				
Wednesday				
Thursday				
Friday				
Saturday				
Sanday				
Total				

Week 2	General (transport, food, medicine, etc)	Rest (entertaiment, restaurant, club, etc)	Culture (books, education, exhibition, etc)	Unexpected (gifts, repairs, etc)
Monday				
Tuesday				
Wednesday				
Thursday				
Friday				
Saturday				
Sanday				
Total				

Week 3	General (transport, food, medicine, etc)	Rest (entertaiment, restaurant, club, etc)	Culture (books, education, exhibition, etc)	Unexpected (gifts, repairs, etc)
Monday				
Tuesday				
Wednesday				
Thursday				
Friday				
Saturday				
Sanday				
Total				

Week 4	General (transport, food, medicine, etc)	Rest (entertaiment, restaurant, club, etc)	Culture (books, education, exhibition, etc)	Unexpected (gifts, repairs, etc)
Monday				
Tuesday				
Wednesday				
Thursday				
Friday				
Saturday				
Sanday				
Total				

Week 5	General (transport, food, medicine, etc)	Rest (entertaiment, restaurant, club, etc)	Culture (books, education, exhibition, etc)	Unexpected (gifts, repairs, etc)
Monday				
Tuesday				
Wednesday				
Thursday				
Friday				
Saturday				
Sanday				
Total				

Week 6	General (transport, food, medicine, etc)	Rest (entertaiment, restaurant, club, etc)	Culture (books, education, exhibition, etc)	Unexpected (gifts, repairs, etc)
Monday				
Tuesday				
Total				

	General	Rest	Culture	Unexpected
Week 1				
Week 2				
Week 3				
Week 4				
Week 5				
Week 6				
Total				

Month total $_{T7}$

Free Money $_{T3}$ — Month total $_{T7}$ = Save Money

Monthly Income

Source	Data	Amount

Total $_{T1}$

Fixed Monthly Expenses

Mortgage		Bills(Electric,Gas,Water)	
Insurance		Phone	
Credits		Internet	

Total $_{T2}$

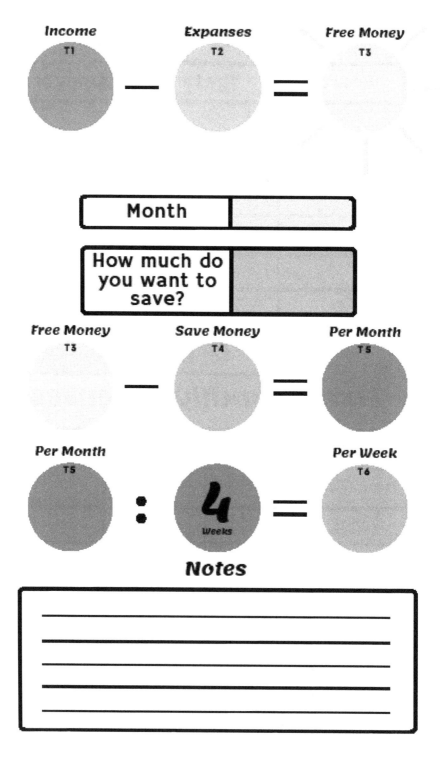

Week 1	General (transport, food, medicine, etc)	Rest (entertaiment, restaurant, club, etc)	Culture (books, education, exhibition, etc)	Unexpected (gifts, repairs, etc)
Monday				
Tuesday				
Wednesday				
Thursday				
Friday				
Saturday				
Sanday				
Total				

Week **2**	**General** (transport, food, medicine, etc)	**Rest** (entertaiment, restaurant, club, etc)	**Culture** (books, education, exhibition, etc)	**Unexpected** (gifts, repairs, etc)
Monday				
Tuesday				
Wednesday				
Thursday				
Friday				
Saturday				
Sanday				
Total				

Week 3	General (transport, food, medicine, etc)	Rest (entertaiment, restaurant, club, etc)	Culture (books, education, exhibition, etc)	Unexpected (gifts, repairs, etc)
Monday				
Tuesday				
Wednesday				
Thursday				
Friday				
Saturday				
Sanday				
Total				

Week 4	General (transport, food, medicine, etc)	Rest (entertaiment, restaurant, club, etc)	Culture (books, education, exhibition, etc)	Unexpected (gifts, repairs, etc)
Monday				
Tuesday				
Wednesday				
Thursday				
Friday				
Saturday				
Sanday				
Total				

Week 5	General (transport, food, medicine, etc)	Rest (entertaiment, restaurant, club, etc)	Culture (books, education, exhibition, etc)	Unexpected (gifts, repairs, etc)
Monday				
Tuesday				
Wednesday				
Thursday				
Friday				
Saturday				
Sanday				
Total				

Week 6	General (transport, food, medicine, etc)	Rest (entertaiment, restaurant, club, etc)	Culture (books, education, exhibition, etc)	Unexpected (gifts, repairs, etc)
Monday				
Tuesday				
Total				

	General	Rest	Culture	Unexpected
Week 1				
Week 2				
Week 3				
Week 4				
Week 5				
Week 6				
Total				

Month total $_{T7}$

Free Money $_{T3}$ — Month total $_{T7}$ = Save Money

month

12

Monthly Income

Source	Data	Amount

Total $_{T1}$

Fixed Monthly Expenses

Mortgage		Bills(Electric, Gas, Water)	
Insurance		Phone	
Credits		Internet	

Total $_{T2}$

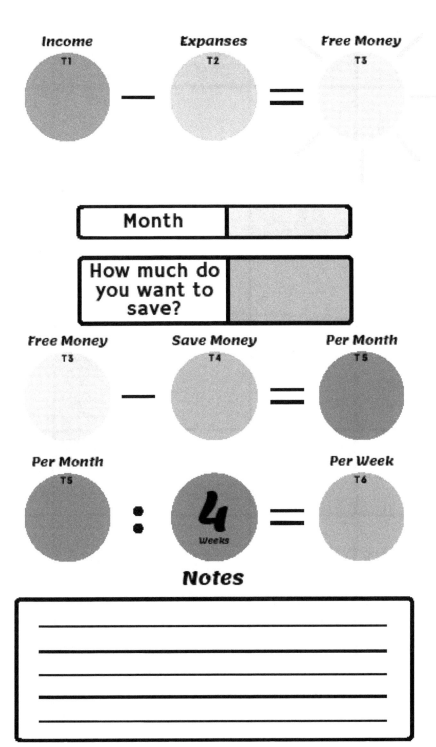

Week 1	General (transport, food, medicine, etc)	Rest (entertaiment, restaurant, club, etc)	Culture (books, education, exhibition, etc)	Unexpected (gifts, repairs, etc)
Monday				
Tuesday				
Wednesday				
Thursday				
Friday				
Saturday				
Sanday				
Total				

Week 2	General (transport, food, medicine, etc)	Rest (entertaiment, restaurant, club, etc)	Culture (books, education, exhibition, etc)	Unexpected (gifts, repairs, etc)
Monday				
Tuesday				
Wednesday				
Thursday				
Friday				
Saturday				
Sanday				
Total				

Week 3	General (transport, food, medicine, etc)	Rest (entertaiment, restaurant, club, etc)	Culture (books, education, exhibition, etc)	Unexpected (gifts, repairs, etc)
Monday				
Tuesday				
Wednesday				
Thursday				
Friday				
Saturday				
Sanday				
Total				

Week 4	General (transport, food, medicine, etc)	Rest (entertaiment, restaurant, club, etc)	Culture (books, education, exhibition, etc)	Unexpected (gifts, repairs, etc)
Monday				
Tuesday				
Wednesday				
Thursday				
Friday				
Saturday				
Sanday				
Total				

Week 5	General (transport, food, medicine, etc)	Rest (entertaiment, restaurant, club, etc)	Culture (books, education, exhibition, etc)	Unexpected (gifts, repairs, etc)
Monday				
Tuesday				
Wednesday				
Thursday				
Friday				
Saturday				
Sanday				
Total				

Week 6	General (transport, food, medicine, etc)	Rest (entertaiment, restaurant, club, etc)	Culture (books, education, exhibition, etc)	Unexpected (gifts, repairs, etc)
Monday				
Tuesday				
Total				

	General	Rest	Culture	Unexpected
Week 1				
Week 2				
Week 3				
Week 4				
Week 5				
Week 6				
Total				

Month total $_{T7}$

Free Money $_{T3}$ — Month total $_{T7}$ = Save Money

CPSIA information can be obtained
at www.ICGtesting.com
Printed in the USA
LVHW050429291121
704718LV00027B/1447